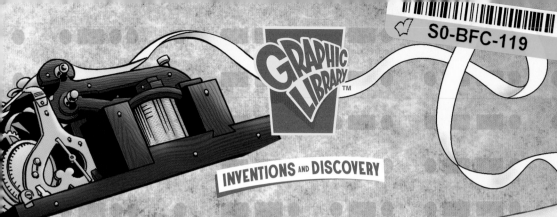

GRAPHIC LIBRARY™

INVENTIONS AND DISCOVERY

Samuel Morse and the TELEGRAPH

by David Seidman

illustrated by Rod Whigham and Charles Barnett III

Consultant:
Tom Perera PhD
Professor Emeritus
Montclair State University
Upper Montclair, New Jersey

Capstone

Mankato, Minnesota

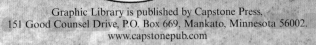

Graphic Library is published by Capstone Press,
151 Good Counsel Drive, P.O. Box 669, Mankato, Minnesota 56002.
www.capstonepub.com

Printed in the United States of America in Stevens Point, Wisconsin.

072012
006841CPS

Books published by Capstone Press are manufactured with paper containing at least 10 percent post-consumer waste.

Library of Congress Cataloging-in-Publication Data
Seidman, David, 1959–
Samuel Morse and the telegraph / by David Seidman; illustrated by Rod Whigham and Charles Barnett III.
p. cm.—(Graphic library. Inventions and discovery)
Summary: "In graphic novel format, tells the story of how Samuel Morse developed a working telegraph in 1844 that changed the way people communicated"—Provided by publisher.
Includes bibliographical references and index.
ISBN-13: 978-0-7368-6846-4 (hardcover)
ISBN-10: 0-7368-6846-1 (hardcover)
ISBN-13: 978-0-7368-7898-2 (softcover pbk.)
ISBN-10: 0-7368-7898-X (softcover pbk.)
1. Morse, Samuel Finley Breese, 1791–1872—Juvenile literature. 2. Inventors—United States—Biography—Juvenile literature. I. Title. II. Series.
TK5243.M7S45 2007
621.383'092—dc22
[B] 2006024906

Designers
Alison Thiele and Ted Williams

Production *Designer*
Kim Brown

Colorist
Tami Collins

Editor
Christine Peterson

The author dedicates this book to Will Eisner and Larry Gonick, who pioneered nonfiction comics.

The Morse code used in artwork in this book is the American Morse code developed by Samuel Morse in 1838.

Editor's note: Direct quotations from primary sources are indicated by a yellow background.

Direct quotations appear on the following pages:
Page 6, from an August 17, 1811, letter by Morse; page 14, from a letter by Morse dated October 14, 1837; part of the Samuel F. B. Morse Papers at the Library of Congress (http://memory.loc.gov/ammem/sfbmhtml/sfbmhome.html).
Pages 9 and 16, from *Samuel F. B. Morse: His Letters and Journals*, edited by Edward Lind Morse (Boston: Houghton Mifflin, 1914).
Page 15, quotes attributed to Samuel Morse and Annie Ellsworth as published in *The American Leonardo: A Life of Samuel F. B. Morse* by Carleton Mabee (New York: A. A. Knopf, 1943).
Page 19, from the U.S. Supreme Court case *O'Reilly versus Morse* (http://supreme.justia.com/us/56/62/case.html).
Page 21, quote attributed to Charles Minot as published in *When Railroads Were New* by Charles Frederick Carter (New York: H. Holt, 1909).

Table of "•••"'•'•"•"" CONTENTS

Chapter 1

The Need for Speed   4

Chapter 2

An Electric Idea   8

Chapter 3

Big Business 18

Chapter 4

Father of the
Modern World 24

More about Morse
and the Telegraph 28
Glossary 30
Internet Sites 30
Read More 31
Bibliography 31
Index 32

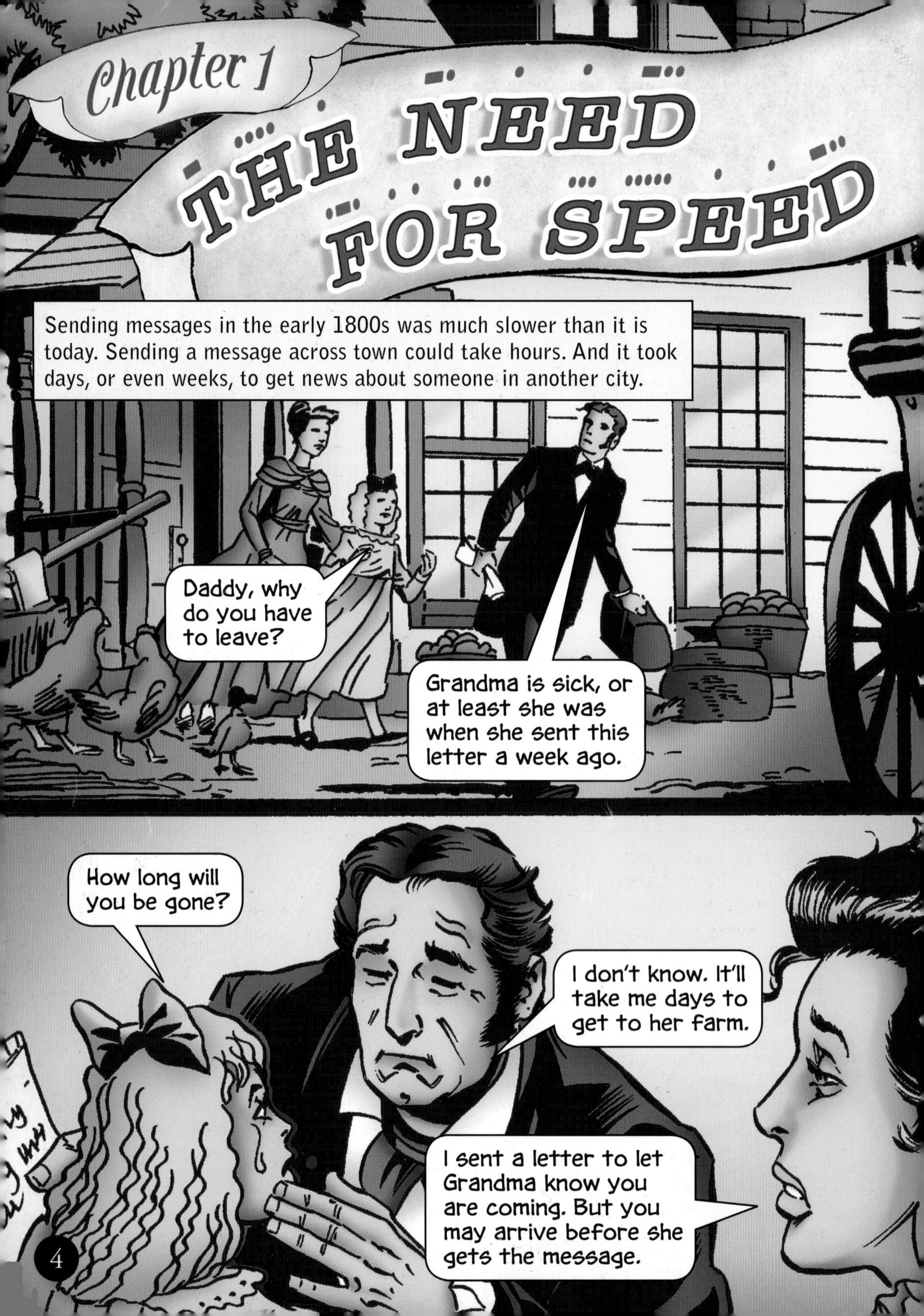
Chapter 1
THE NEED FOR SPEED
Sending messages in the early 1800s was much slower than it is today. Sending a message across town could take hours. And it took days, or even weeks, to get news about someone in another city.
Daddy, why do you have to leave?
Grandma is sick, or at least she was when she sent this letter a week ago.
How long will you be gone?
I don't know. It'll take me days to get to her farm.
I sent a letter to let Grandma know you are coming. But you may arrive before she gets the message.

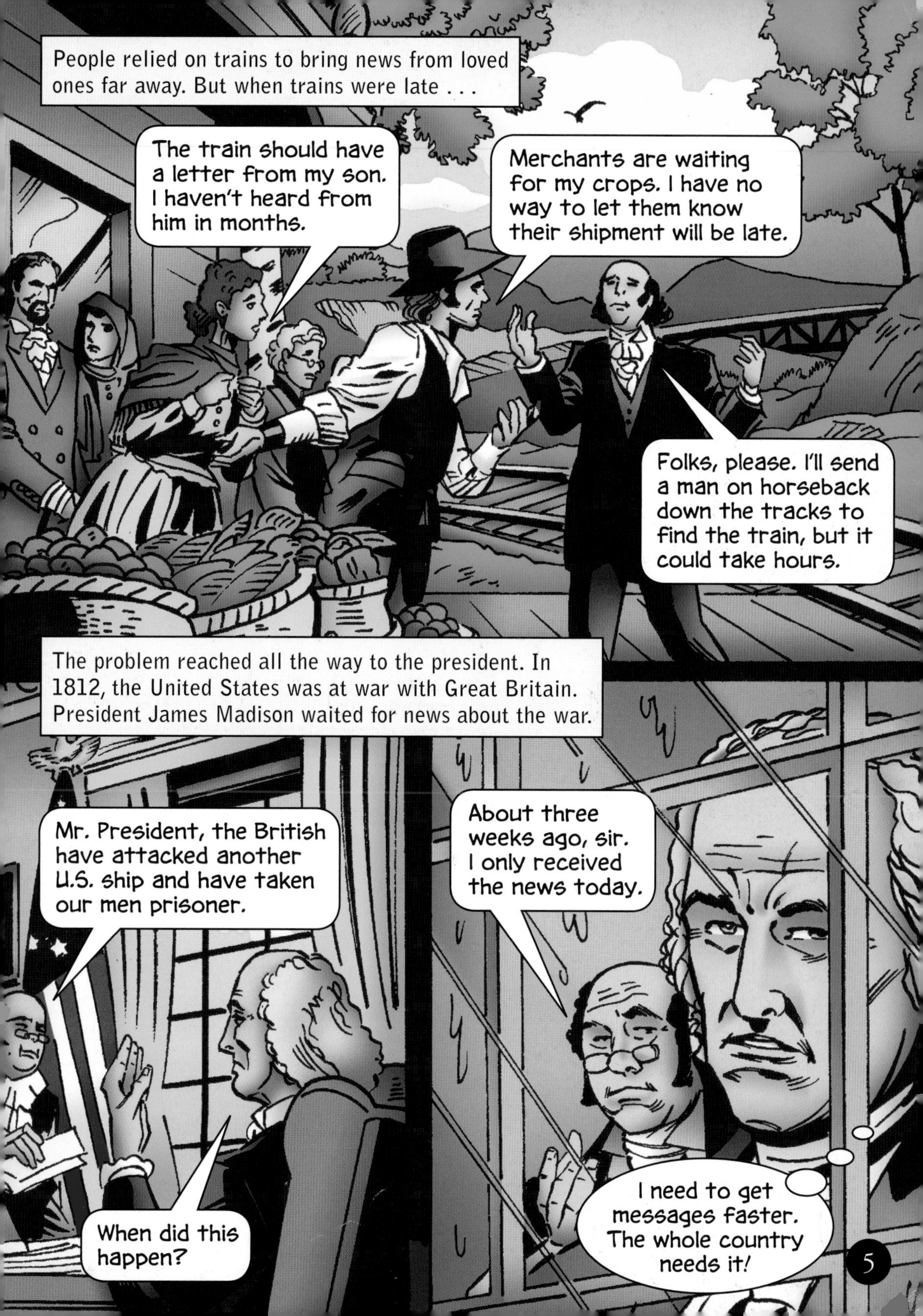
People relied on trains to bring news from loved ones far away. But when trains were late . . .
The train should have a letter from my son. I haven't heard from him in months.
Merchants are waiting for my crops. I have no way to let them know their shipment will be late.
Folks, please. I'll send a man on horseback down the tracks to find the train, but it could take hours.
The problem reached all the way to the president. In 1812, the United States was at war with Great Britain. President James Madison waited for news about the war.
Mr. President, the British have attacked another U.S. ship and have taken our men prisoner.
When did this happen?
About three weeks ago, sir. I only received the news today.
I need to get messages faster. The whole country needs it!

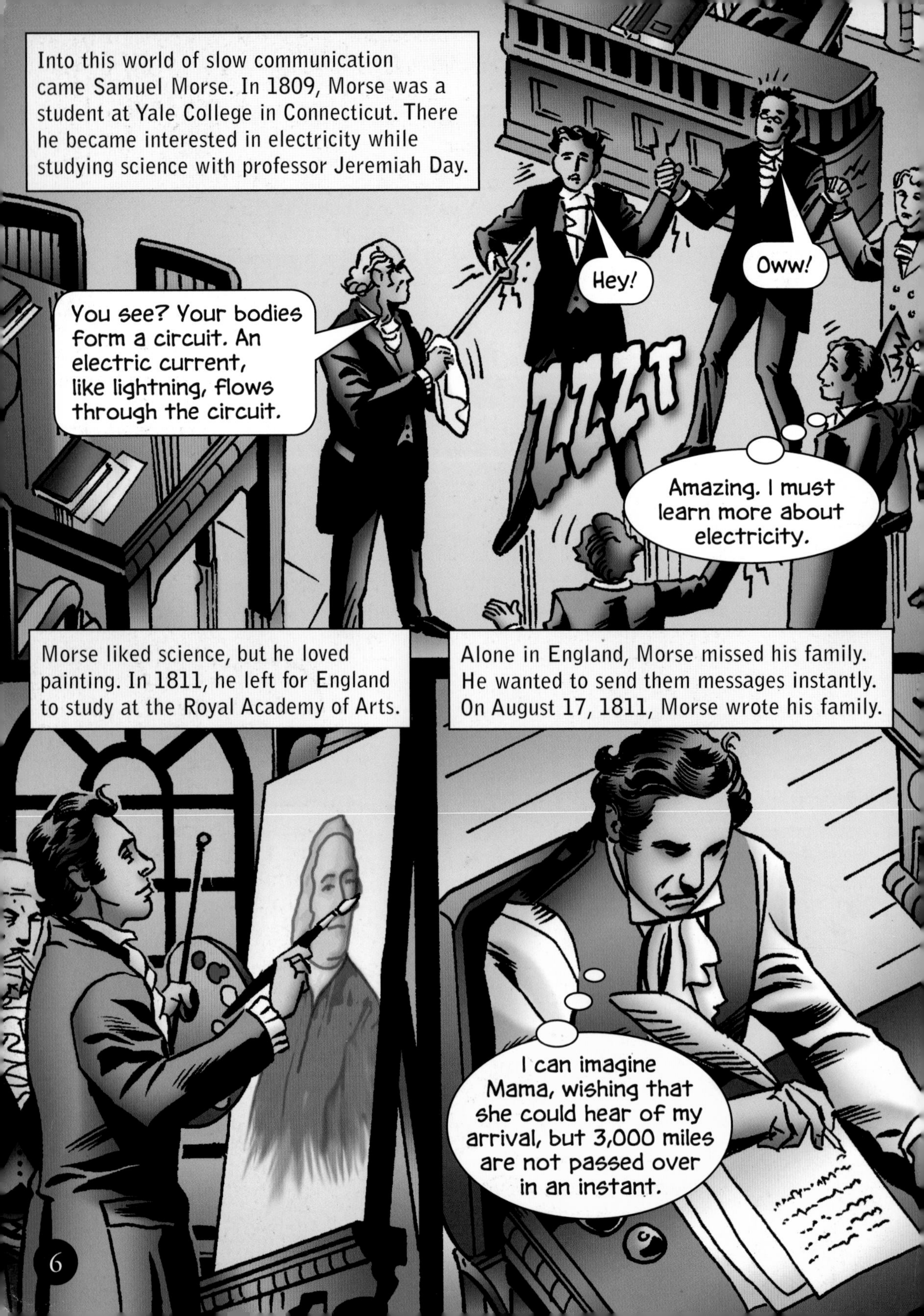
Into this world of slow communication came Samuel Morse. In 1809, Morse was a student at Yale College in Connecticut. There he became interested in electricity while studying science with professor Jeremiah Day.
You see? Your bodies form a circuit. An electric current, like lightning, flows through the circuit.
Hey!
Oww!
ZZZT
Amazing. I must learn more about electricity.
Morse liked science, but he loved painting. In 1811, he left for England to study at the Royal Academy of Arts.
Alone in England, Morse missed his family. He wanted to send them messages instantly. On August 17, 1811, Morse wrote his family.
I can imagine Mama, wishing that she could hear of my arrival, but 3,000 miles are not passed over in an instant.

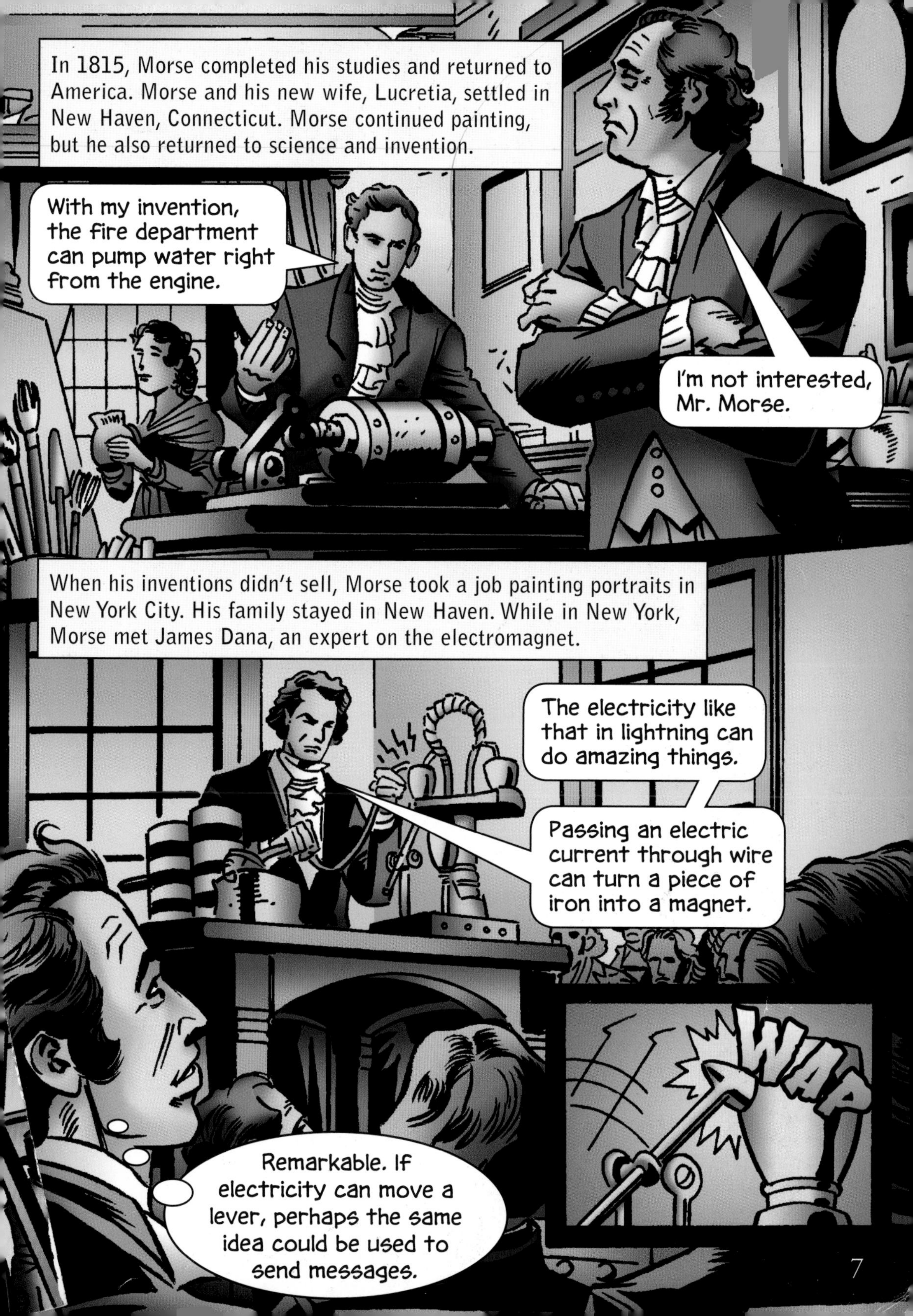
In 1815, Morse completed his studies and returned to America. Morse and his new wife, Lucretia, settled in New Haven, Connecticut. Morse continued painting, but he also returned to science and invention.
With my invention, the fire department can pump water right from the engine.
I'm not interested, Mr. Morse.
When his inventions didn't sell, Morse took a job painting portraits in New York City. His family stayed in New Haven. While in New York, Morse met James Dana, an expert on the electromagnet.
The electricity like that in lightning can do amazing things.
Passing an electric current through wire can turn a piece of iron into a magnet.
WAP
Remarkable. If electricity can move a lever, perhaps the same idea could be used to send messages.

Chapter 2
"AN ELECTRIC IDEA"

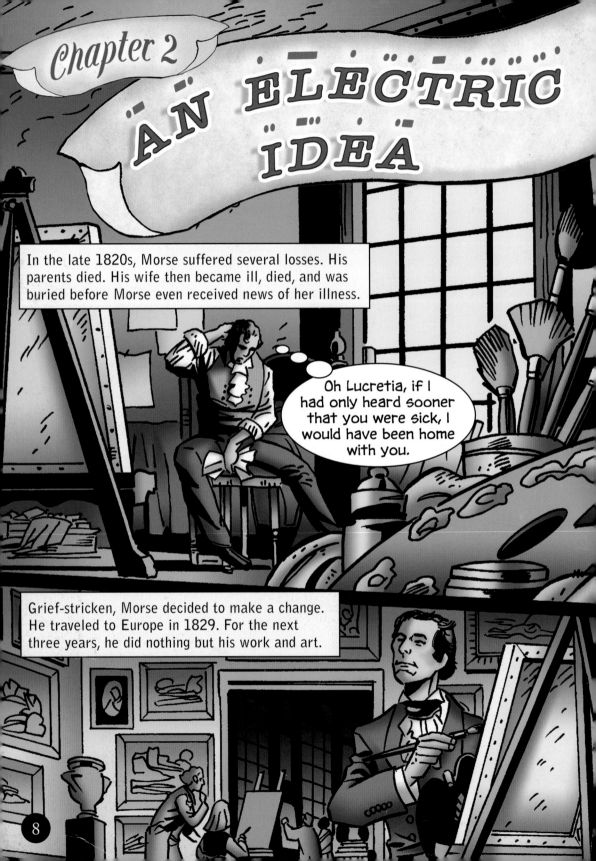

In the late 1820s, Morse suffered several losses. His parents died. His wife then became ill, died, and was buried before Morse even received news of her illness.

Oh Lucretia, if I had only heard sooner that you were sick, I would have been home with you.

Grief-stricken, Morse decided to make a change. He traveled to Europe in 1829. For the next three years, he did nothing but his work and art.

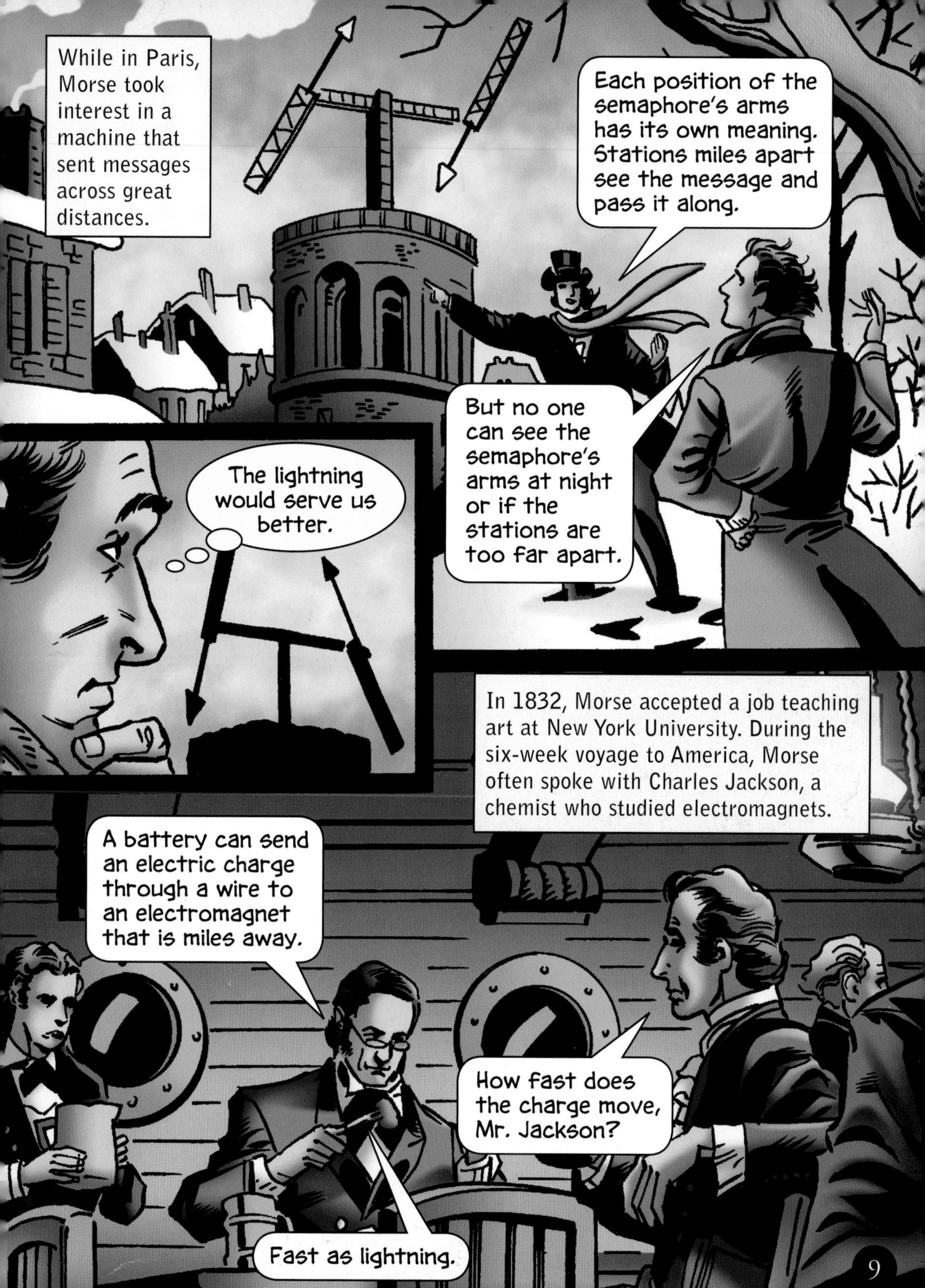
While in Paris, Morse took interest in a machine that sent messages across great distances.
Each position of the semaphore's arms has its own meaning. Stations miles apart see the message and pass it along.
But no one can see the semaphore's arms at night or if the stations are too far apart.
The lightning would serve us better.
In 1832, Morse accepted a job teaching art at New York University. During the six-week voyage to America, Morse often spoke with Charles Jackson, a chemist who studied electromagnets.
A battery can send an electric charge through a wire to an electromagnet that is miles away.
How fast does the charge move, Mr. Jackson?
Fast as lightning.

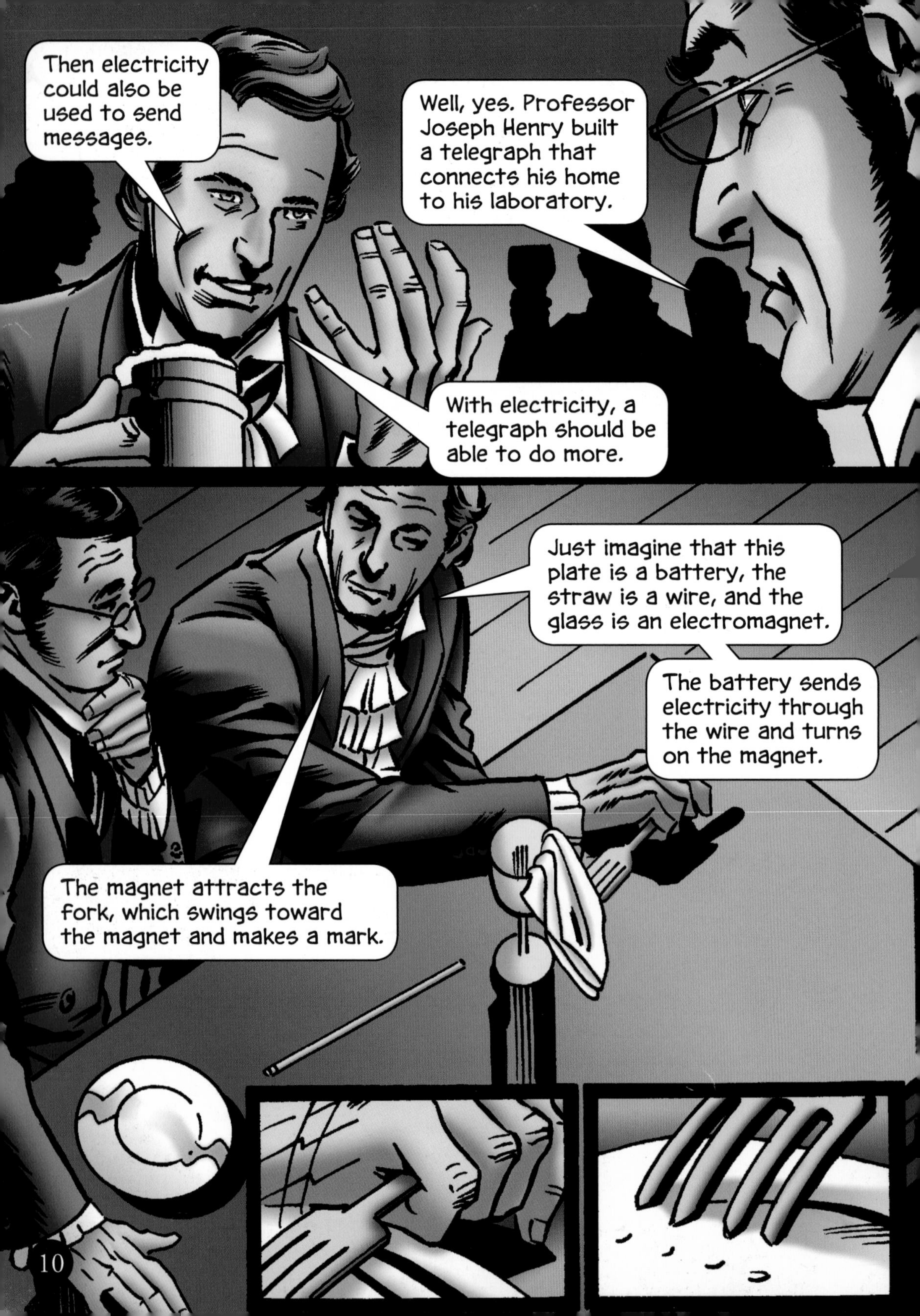
Then electricity could also be used to send messages.
Well, yes. Professor Joseph Henry built a telegraph that connects his home to his laboratory.
With electricity, a telegraph should be able to do more.
Just imagine that this plate is a battery, the straw is a wire, and the glass is an electromagnet.
The battery sends electricity through the wire and turns on the magnet.
The magnet attracts the fork, which swings toward the magnet and makes a mark.

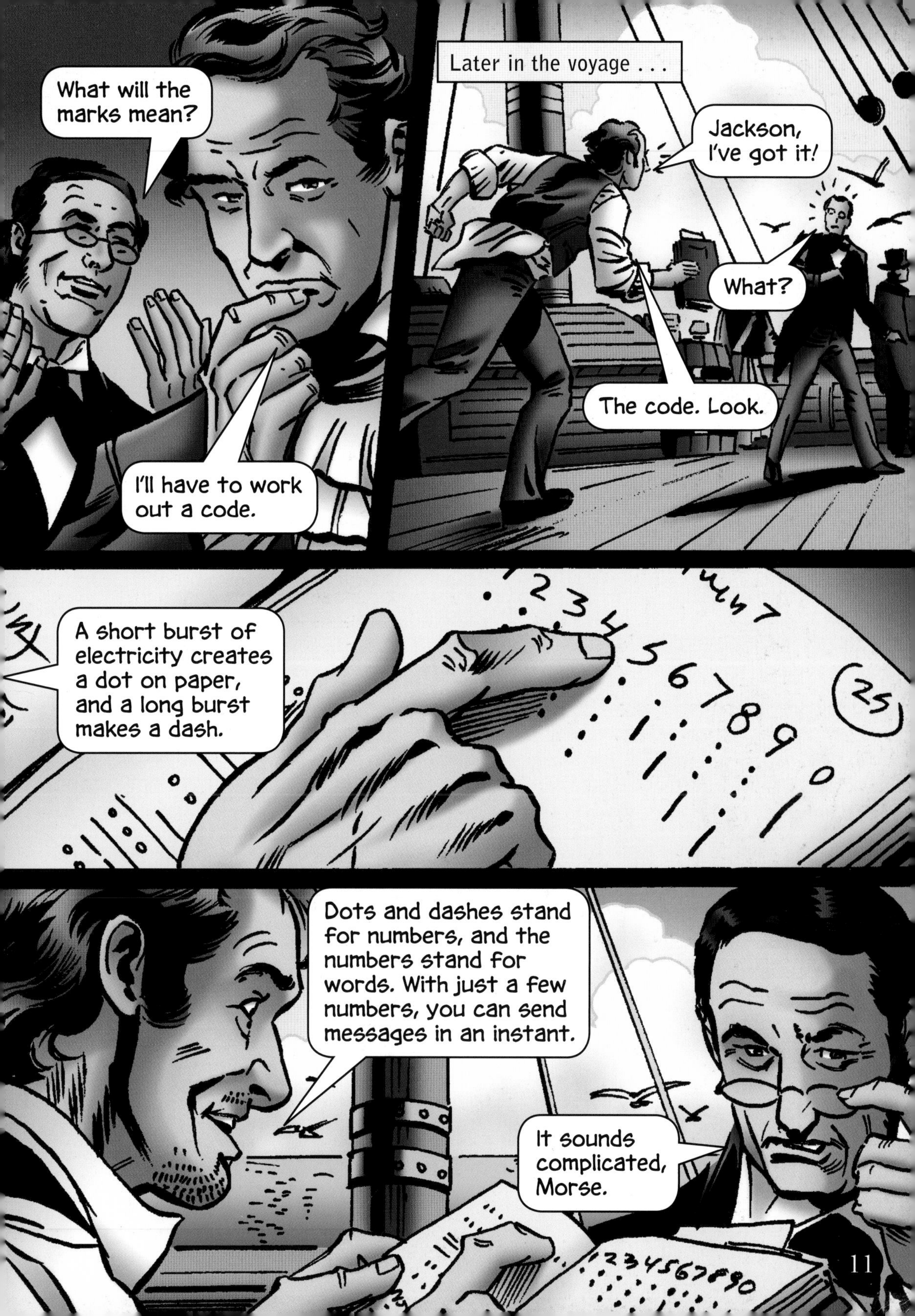
What will the marks mean?
I'll have to work out a code.
Later in the voyage . . .
Jackson, I've got it!
What?
The code. Look.
A short burst of electricity creates a dot on paper, and a long burst makes a dash.
Dots and dashes stand for numbers, and the numbers stand for words. With just a few numbers, you can send messages in an instant.
It sounds complicated, Morse.

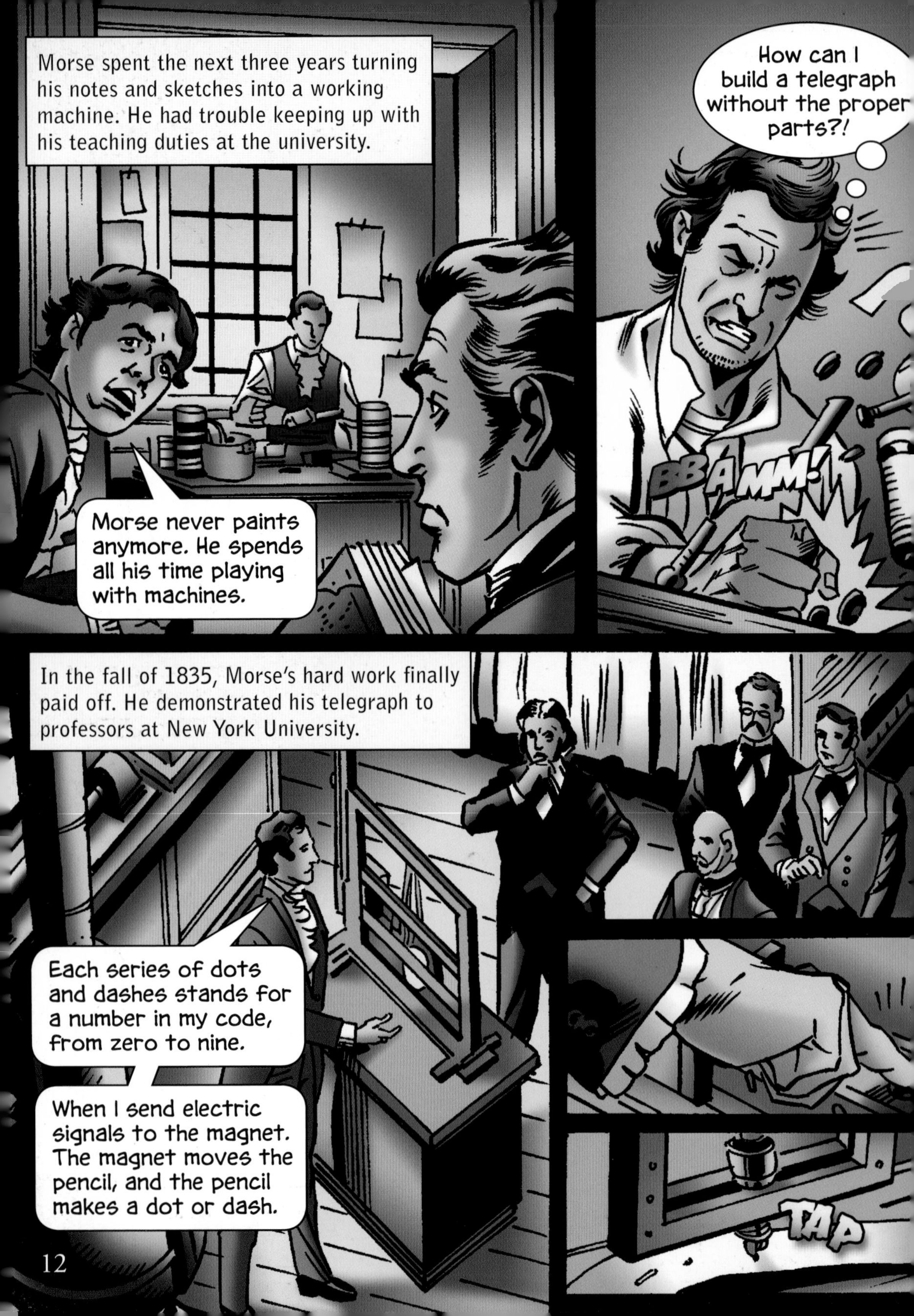

Morse spent the next three years turning his notes and sketches into a working machine. He had trouble keeping up with his teaching duties at the university.
Morse never paints anymore. He spends all his time playing with machines.
How can I build a telegraph without the proper parts?!
BBAMM!
In the fall of 1835, Morse's hard work finally paid off. He demonstrated his telegraph to professors at New York University.
Each series of dots and dashes stands for a number in my code, from zero to nine.
When I send electric signals to the magnet. The magnet moves the pencil, and the pencil makes a dot or dash.
TAP

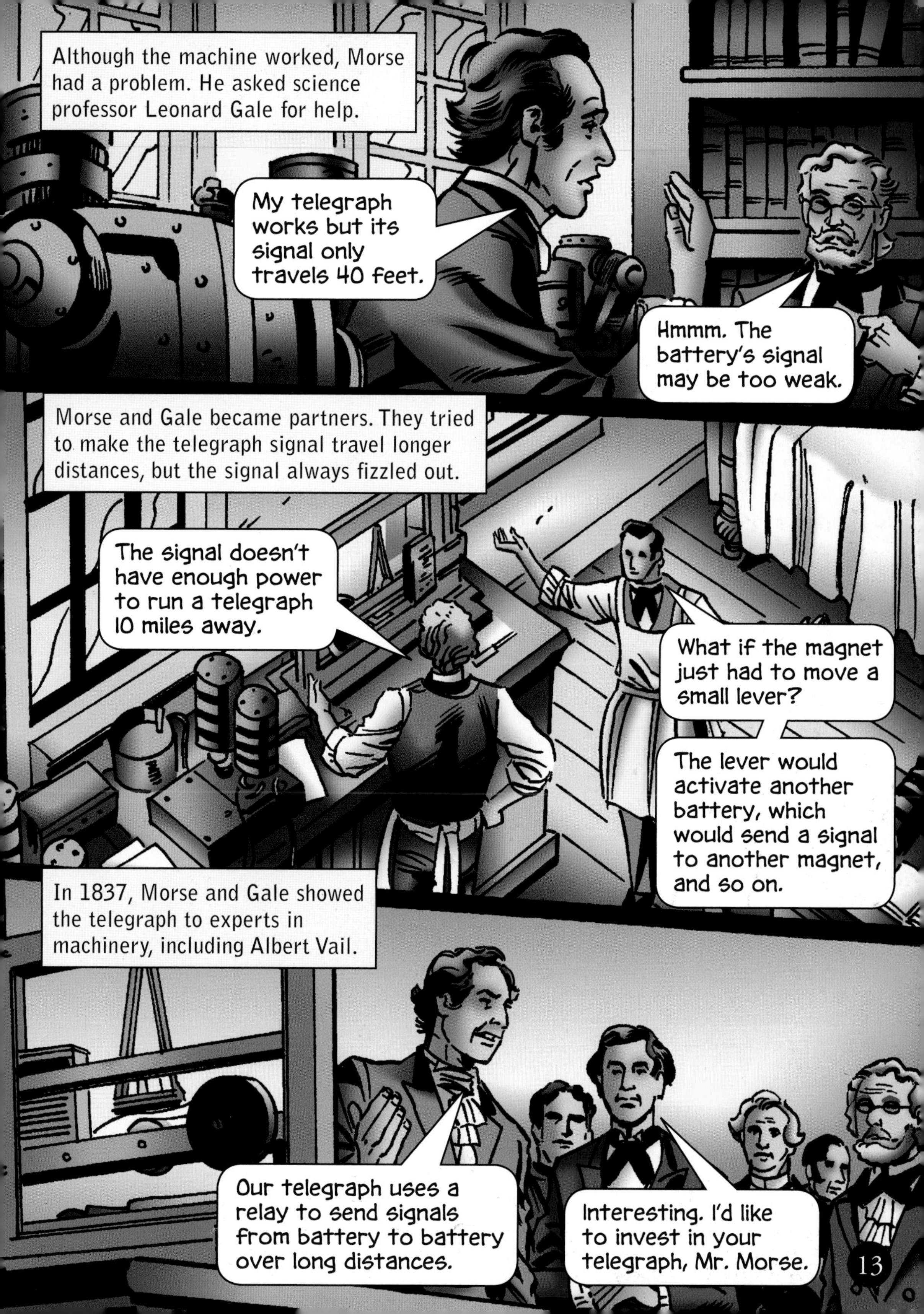
Although the machine worked, Morse had a problem. He asked science professor Leonard Gale for help.
My telegraph works but its signal only travels 40 feet.
Hmmm. The battery's signal may be too weak.
Morse and Gale became partners. They tried to make the telegraph signal travel longer distances, but the signal always fizzled out.
The signal doesn't have enough power to run a telegraph 10 miles away.
What if the magnet just had to move a small lever?
The lever would activate another battery, which would send a signal to another magnet, and so on.
In 1837, Morse and Gale showed the telegraph to experts in machinery, including Albert Vail.
Our telegraph uses a relay to send signals from battery to battery over long distances.
Interesting. I'd like to invest in your telegraph, Mr. Morse.

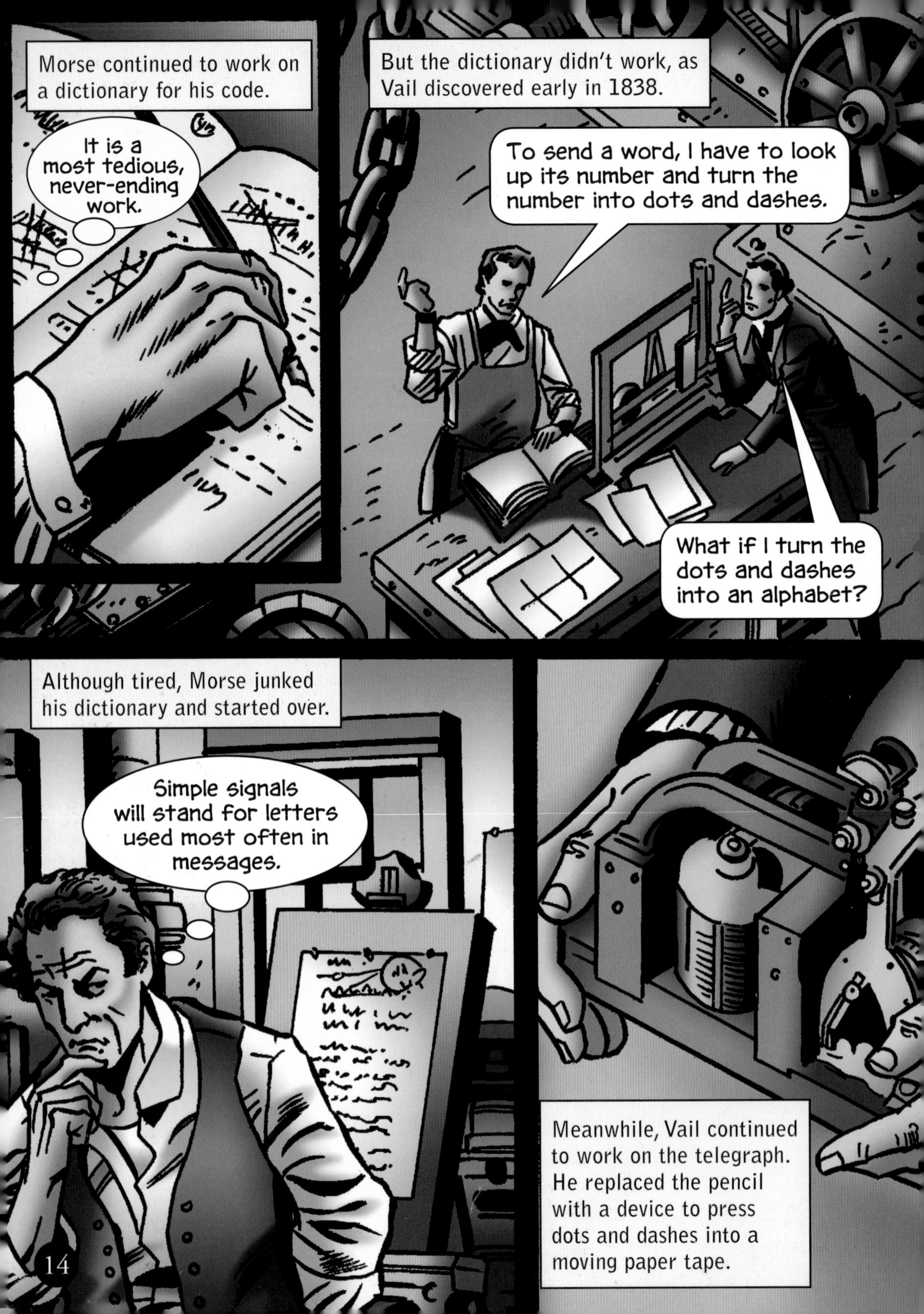
Morse continued to work on a dictionary for his code.
It is a most tedious, never-ending work.
But the dictionary didn't work, as Vail discovered early in 1838.
To send a word, I have to look up its number and turn the number into dots and dashes.
What if I turn the dots and dashes into an alphabet?
Although tired, Morse junked his dictionary and started over.
Simple signals will stand for letters used most often in messages.
Meanwhile, Vail continued to work on the telegraph. He replaced the pencil with a device to press dots and dashes into a moving paper tape.

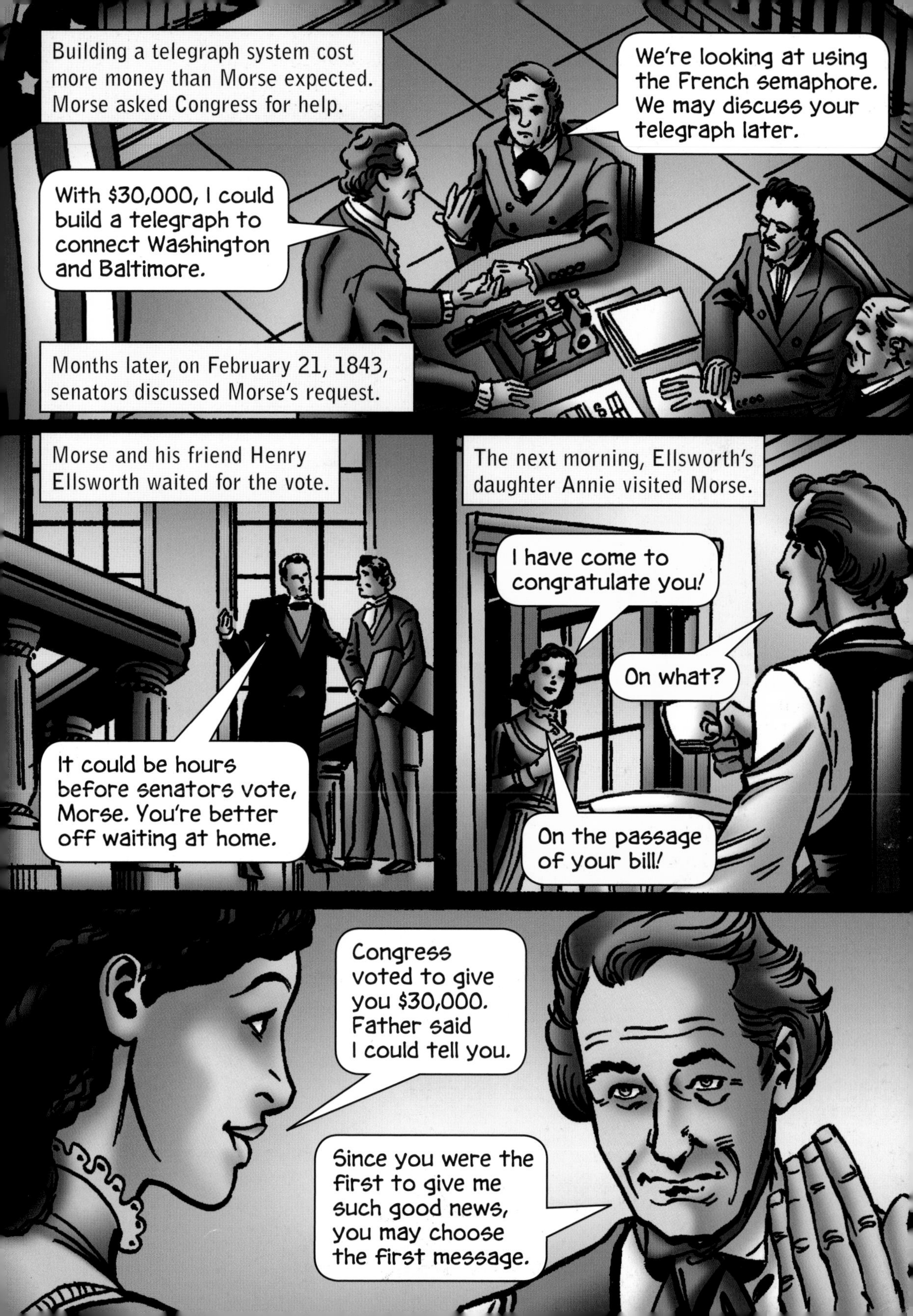
Building a telegraph system cost more money than Morse expected. Morse asked Congress for help.
With $30,000, I could build a telegraph to connect Washington and Baltimore.
We're looking at using the French semaphore. We may discuss your telegraph later.
Months later, on February 21, 1843, senators discussed Morse's request.
Morse and his friend Henry Ellsworth waited for the vote.
It could be hours before senators vote, Morse. You're better off waiting at home.
The next morning, Ellsworth's daughter Annie visited Morse.
I have come to congratulate you!
On what?
On the passage of your bill!
Congress voted to give you $30,000. Father said I could tell you.
Since you were the first to give me such good news, you may choose the first message.

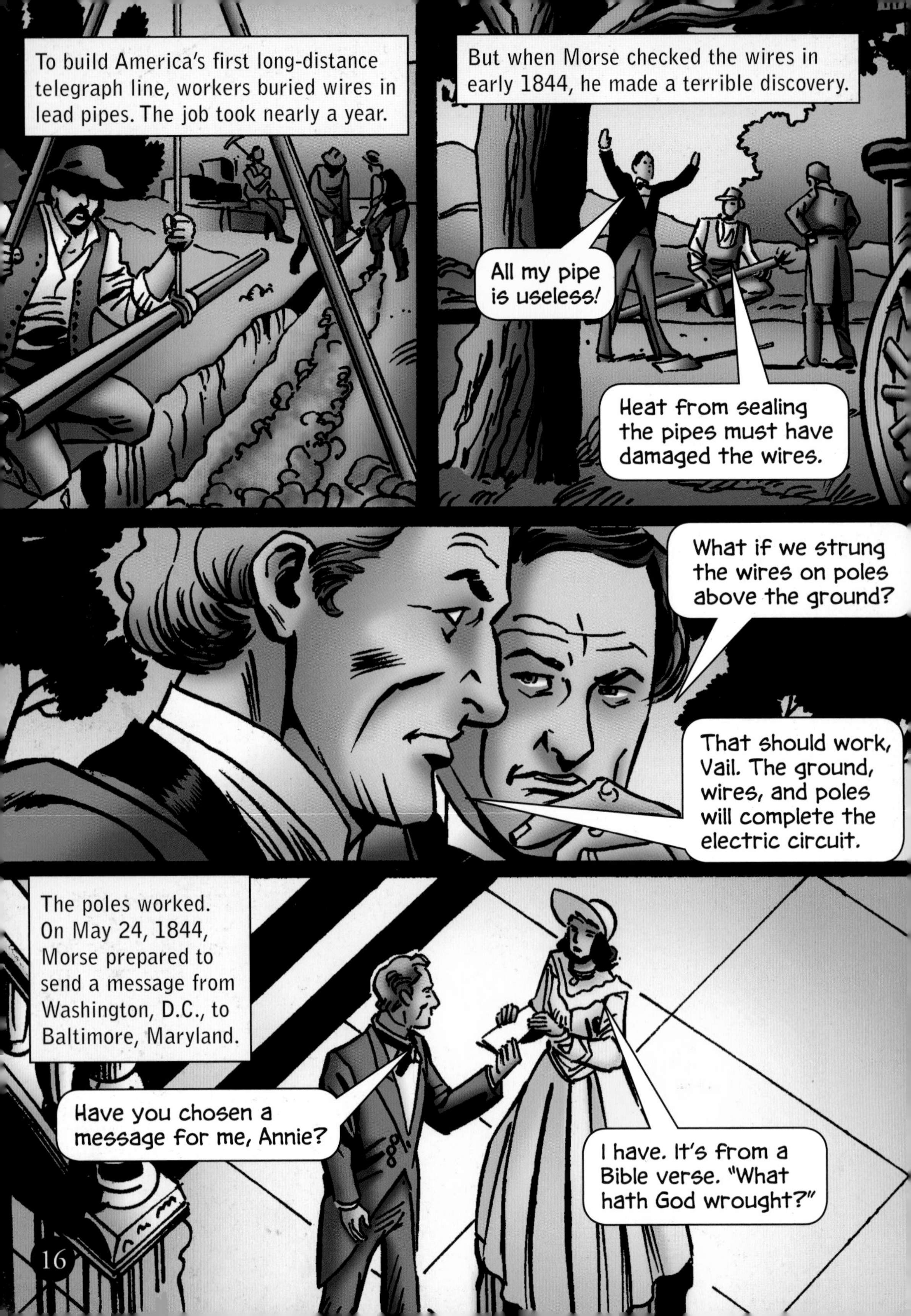
To build America's first long-distance telegraph line, workers buried wires in lead pipes. The job took nearly a year.
But when Morse checked the wires in early 1844, he made a terrible discovery.
All my pipe is useless!
Heat from sealing the pipes must have damaged the wires.
What if we strung the wires on poles above the ground?
That should work, Vail. The ground, wires, and poles will complete the electric circuit.
The poles worked. On May 24, 1844, Morse prepared to send a message from Washington, D.C., to Baltimore, Maryland.
Have you chosen a message for me, Annie?
I have. It's from a Bible verse. "What hath God wrought?"

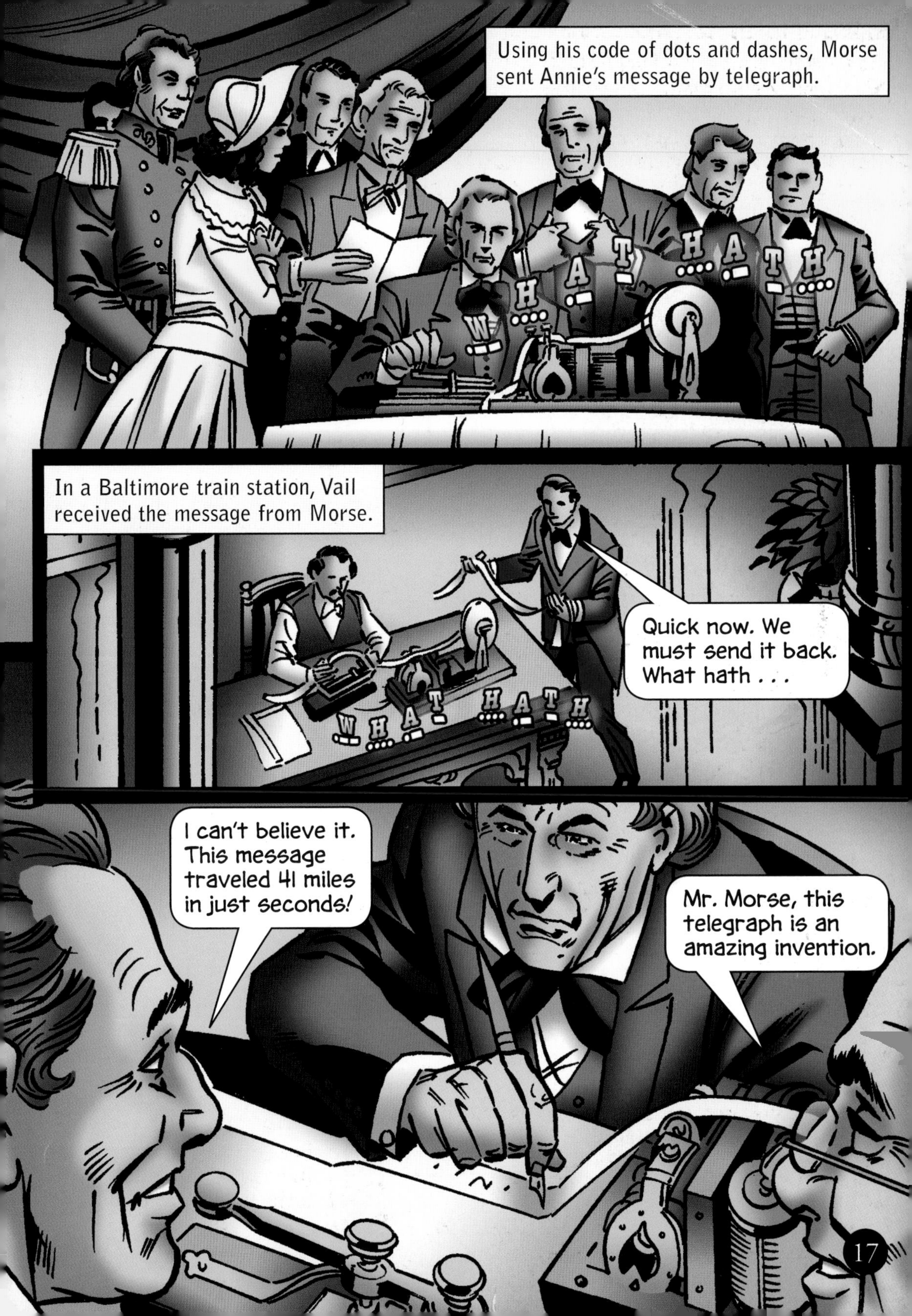
Using his code of dots and dashes, Morse sent Annie's message by telegraph.
In a Baltimore train station, Vail received the message from Morse.
Quick now. We must send it back. What hath . . .
I can't believe it. This message traveled 41 miles in just seconds!
Mr. Morse, this telegraph is an amazing invention.

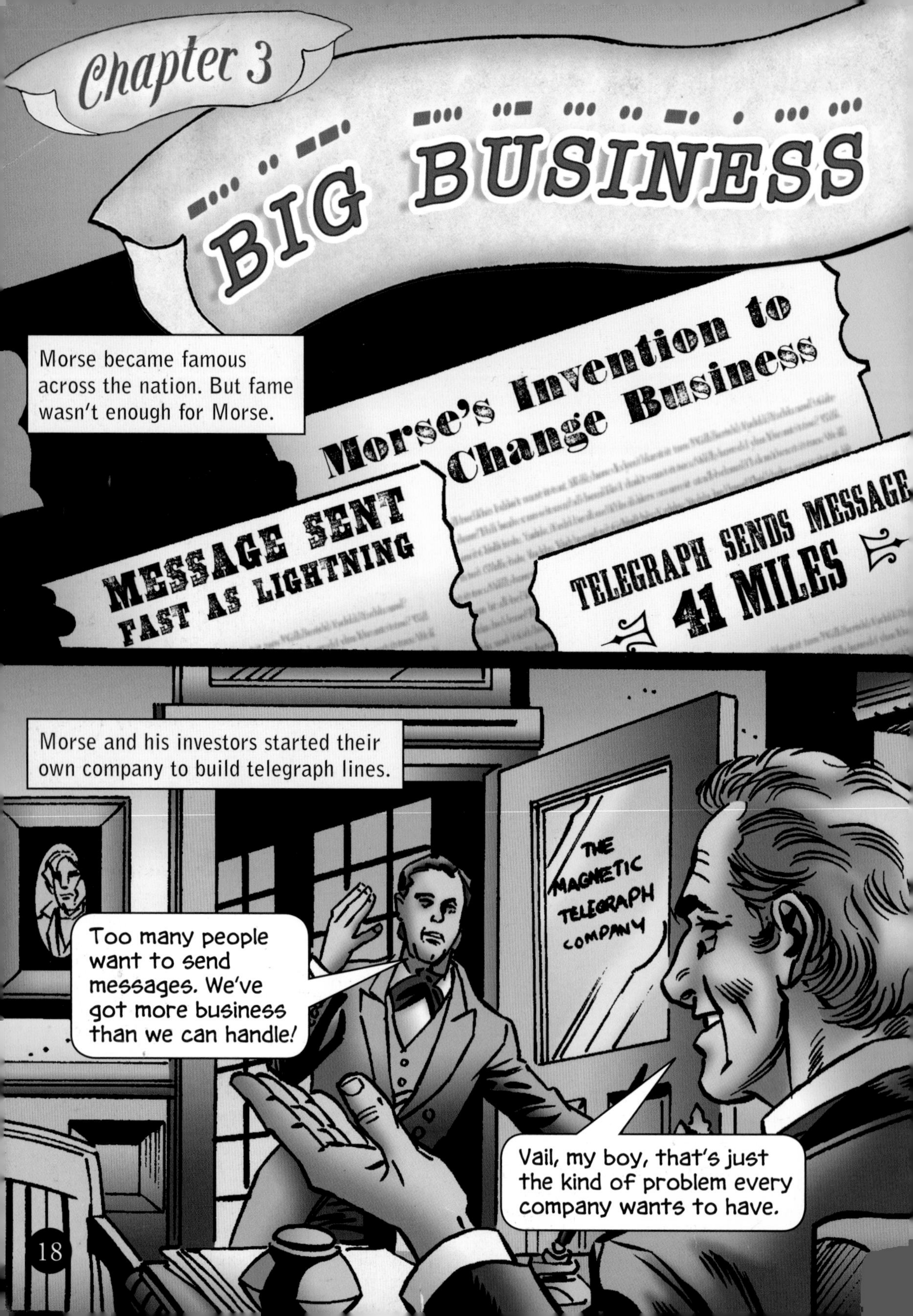

Chapter 3
BIG BUSINESS
Morse became famous across the nation. But fame wasn't enough for Morse.
Morse's Invention to Change Business
MESSAGE SENT FAST AS LIGHTNING
TELEGRAPH SENDS MESSAGE 41 MILES
Morse and his investors started their own company to build telegraph lines.
THE MAGNETIC TELEGRAPH COMPANY
Too many people want to send messages. We've got more business than we can handle!
Vail, my boy, that's just the kind of problem every company wants to have.

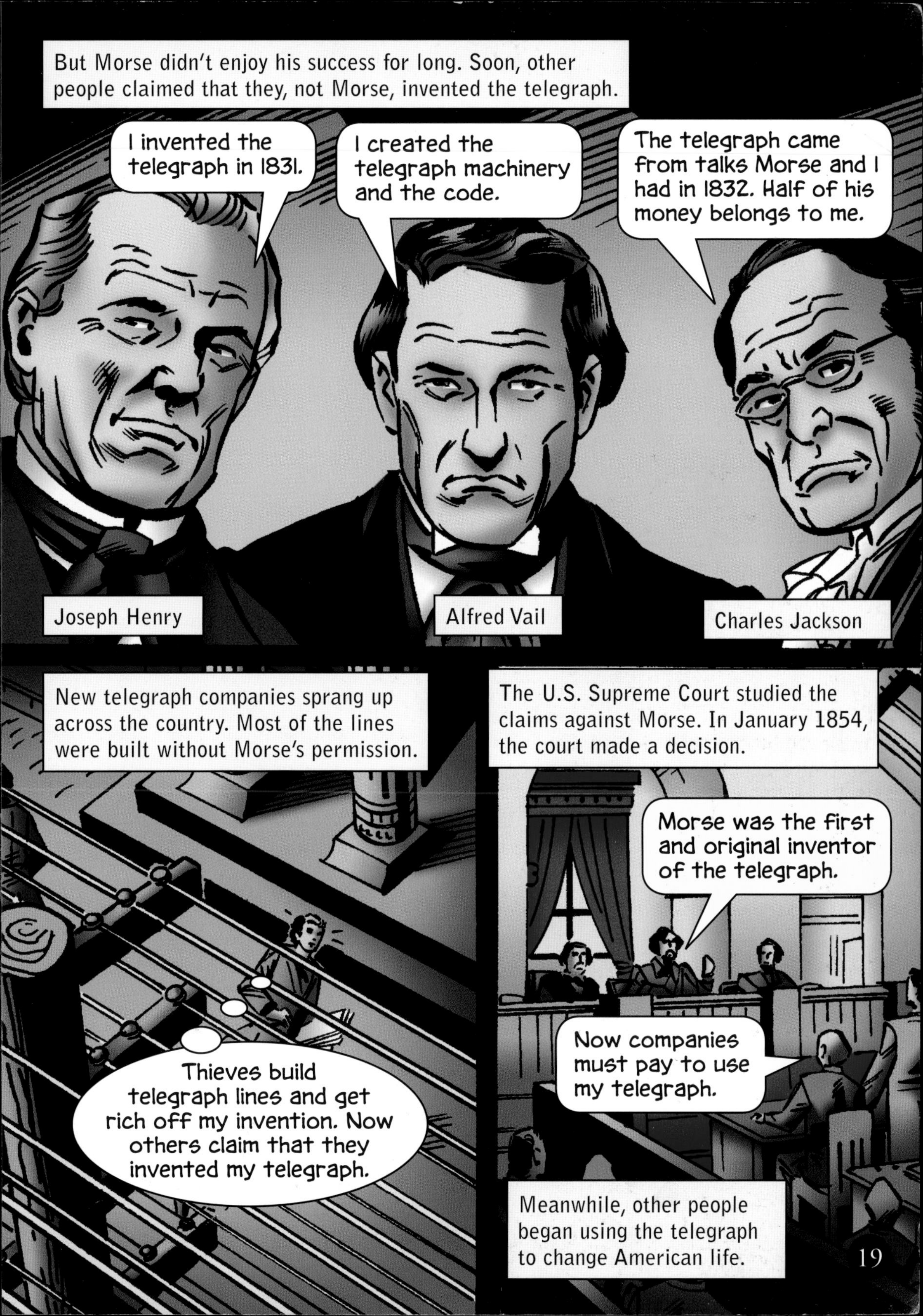
But Morse didn't enjoy his success for long. Soon, other people claimed that they, not Morse, invented the telegraph.
I invented the telegraph in 1831.
I created the telegraph machinery and the code.
The telegraph came from talks Morse and I had in 1832. Half of his money belongs to me.
Joseph Henry
Alfred Vail
Charles Jackson
New telegraph companies sprang up across the country. Most of the lines were built without Morse's permission.
Thieves build telegraph lines and get rich off my invention. Now others claim that they invented my telegraph.
The U.S. Supreme Court studied the claims against Morse. In January 1854, the court made a decision.
Morse was the first and original inventor of the telegraph.
Now companies must pay to use my telegraph.
Meanwhile, other people began using the telegraph to change American life.

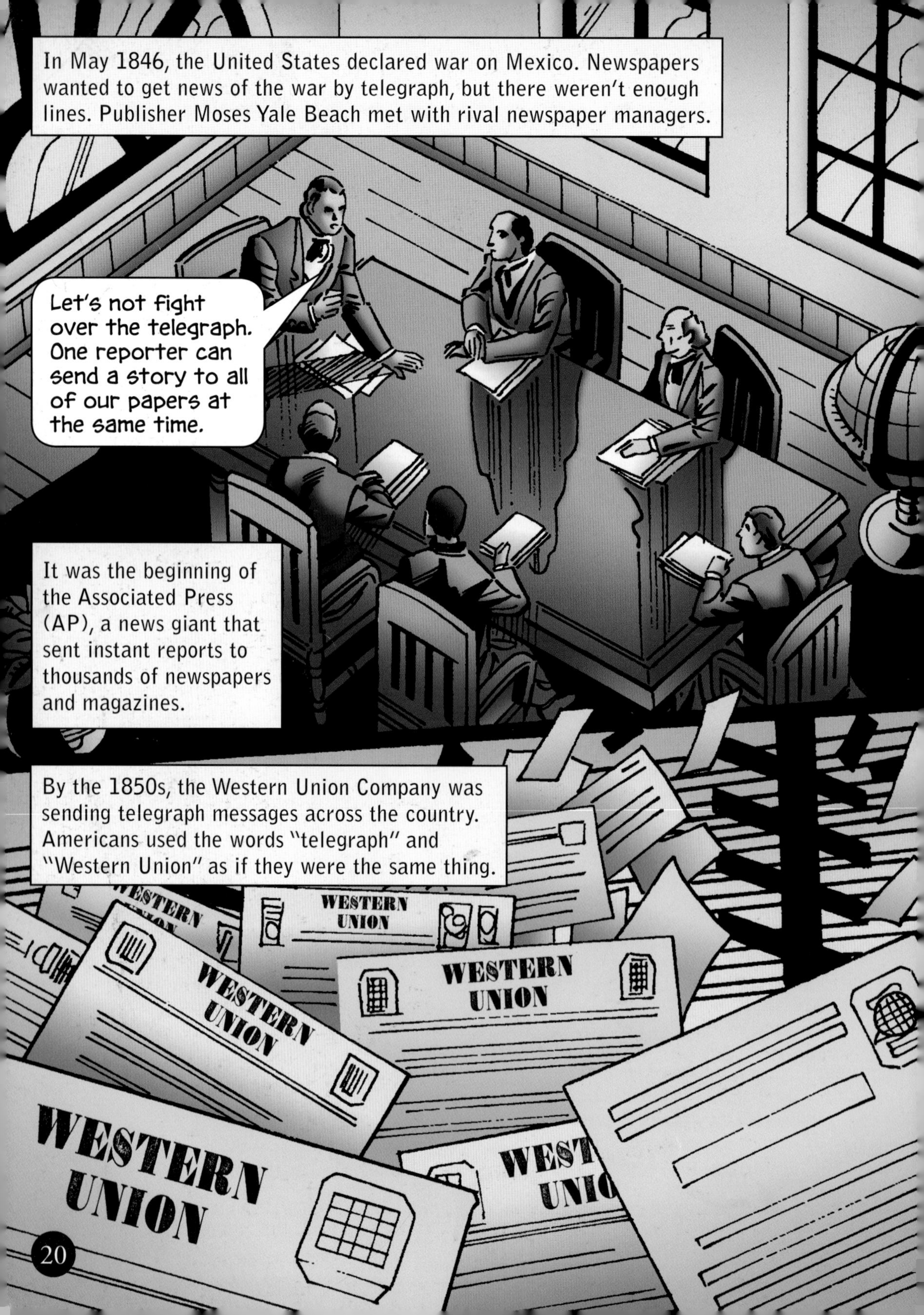
In May 1846, the United States declared war on Mexico. Newspapers wanted to get news of the war by telegraph, but there weren't enough lines. Publisher Moses Yale Beach met with rival newspaper managers.
Let's not fight over the telegraph. One reporter can send a story to all of our papers at the same time.
It was the beginning of the Associated Press (AP), a news giant that sent instant reports to thousands of newspapers and magazines.
By the 1850s, the Western Union Company was sending telegraph messages across the country. Americans used the words "telegraph" and "Western Union" as if they were the same thing.
WESTERN UNION
WESTERN UNION
WESTERN UNION
WESTERN UNION

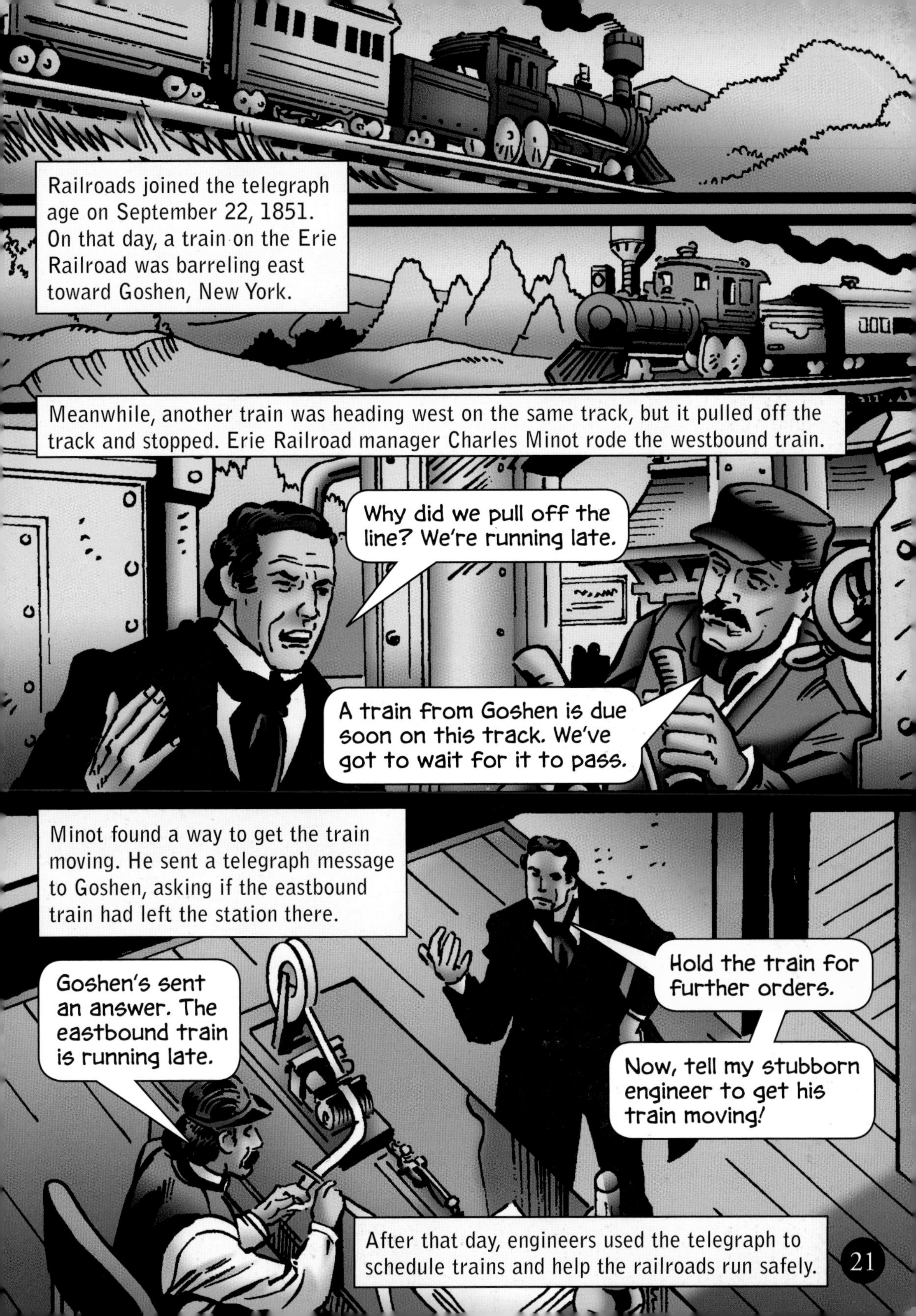
Railroads joined the telegraph age on September 22, 1851. On that day, a train on the Erie Railroad was barreling east toward Goshen, New York.
Meanwhile, another train was heading west on the same track, but it pulled off the track and stopped. Erie Railroad manager Charles Minot rode the westbound train.
Why did we pull off the line? We're running late.
A train from Goshen is due soon on this track. We've got to wait for it to pass.
Minot found a way to get the train moving. He sent a telegraph message to Goshen, asking if the eastbound train had left the station there.
Goshen's sent an answer. The eastbound train is running late.
Hold the train for further orders.
Now, tell my stubborn engineer to get his train moving!
After that day, engineers used the telegraph to schedule trains and help the railroads run safely.

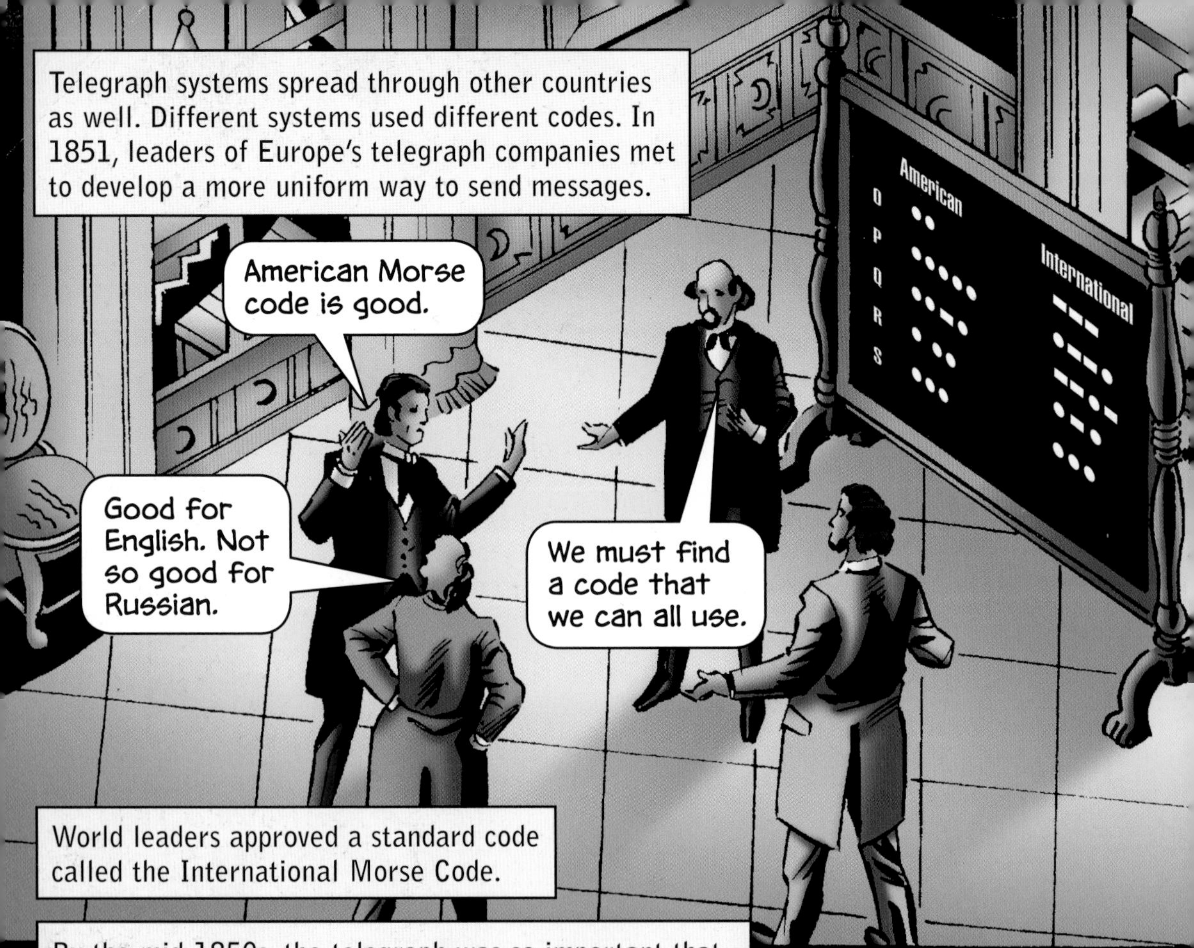
Telegraph systems spread through other countries as well. Different systems used different codes. In 1851, leaders of Europe's telegraph companies met to develop a more uniform way to send messages.
American Morse code is good.
American
International
O
P
Q
R
S
Good for English. Not so good for Russian.
We must find a code that we can all use.
World leaders approved a standard code called the International Morse Code.

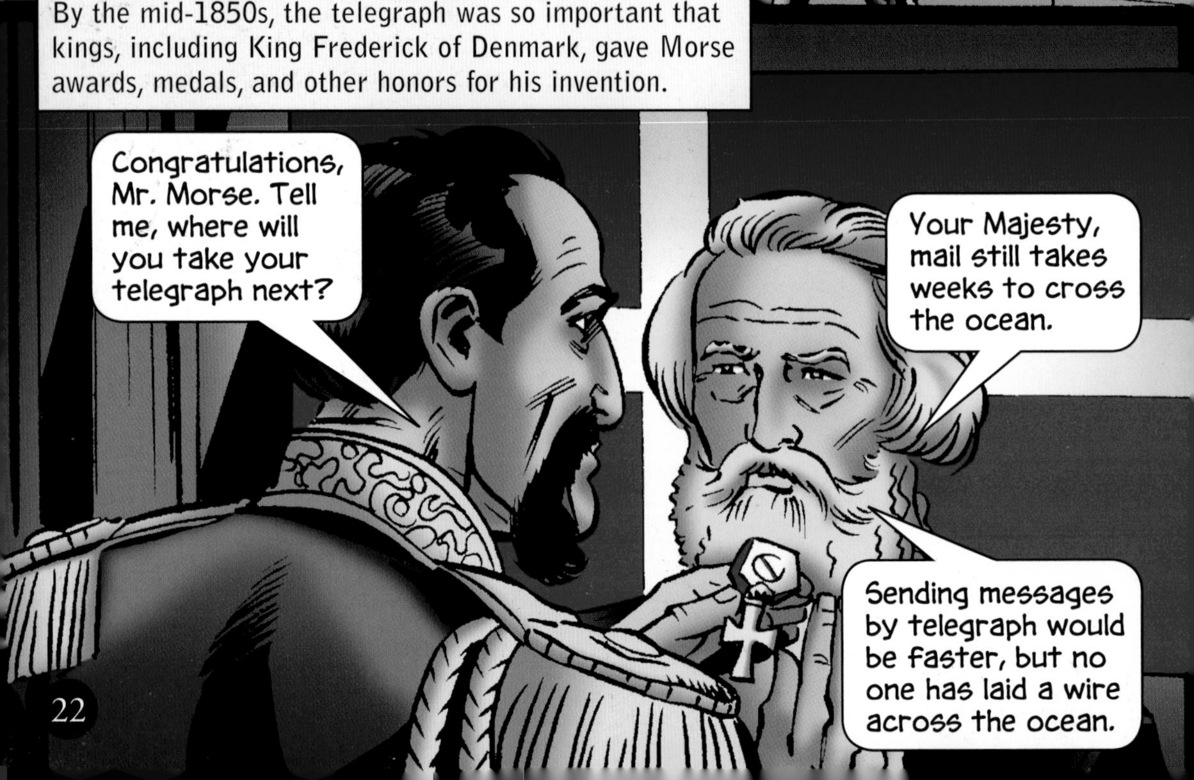
By the mid-1850s, the telegraph was so important that kings, including King Frederick of Denmark, gave Morse awards, medals, and other honors for his invention.
Congratulations, Mr. Morse. Tell me, where will you take your telegraph next?
Your Majesty, mail still takes weeks to cross the ocean.
Sending messages by telegraph would be faster, but no one has laid a wire across the ocean.

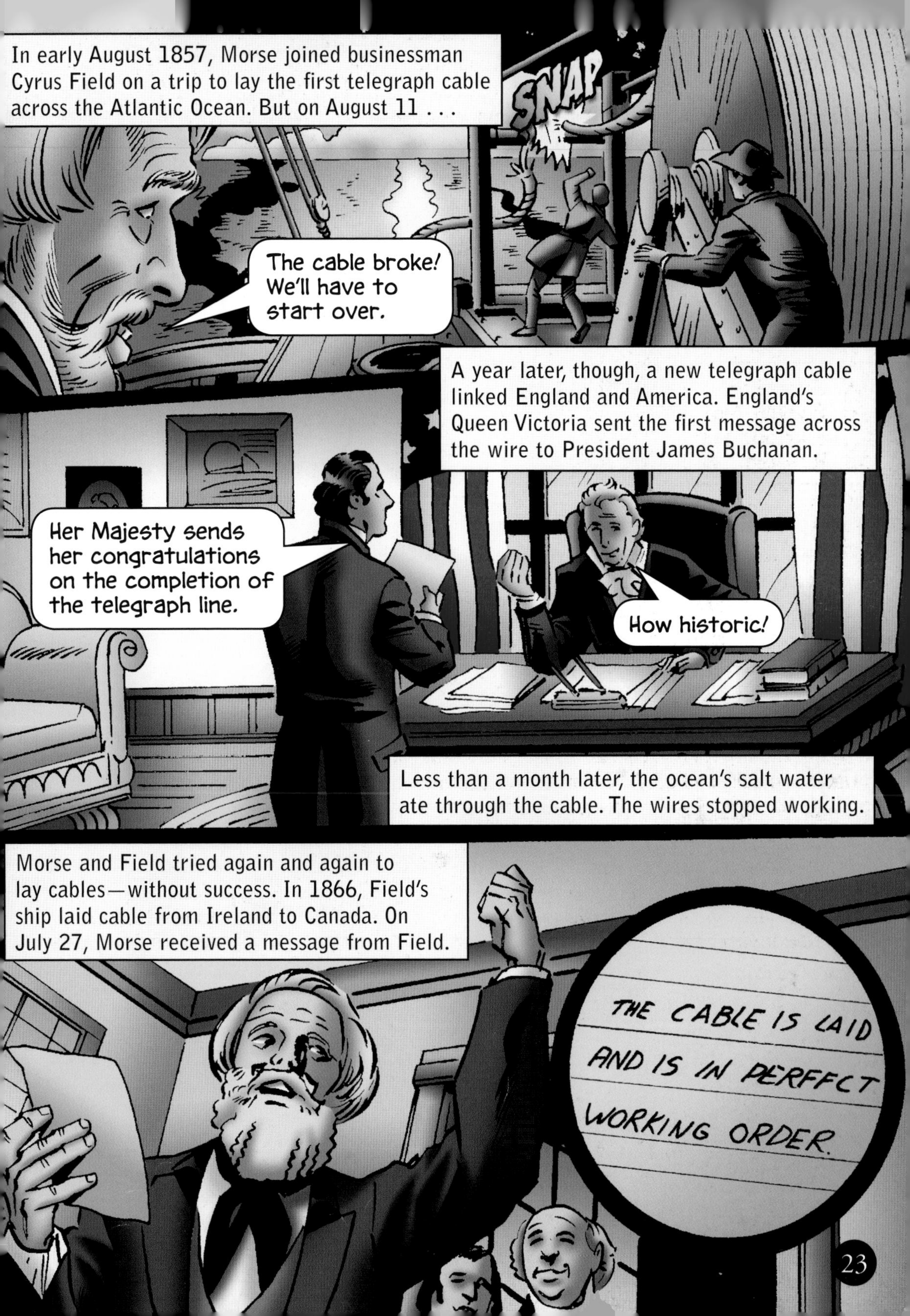
In early August 1857, Morse joined businessman Cyrus Field on a trip to lay the first telegraph cable across the Atlantic Ocean. But on August 11 . . .
SNAP
The cable broke! We'll have to start over.
A year later, though, a new telegraph cable linked England and America. England's Queen Victoria sent the first message across the wire to President James Buchanan.
Her Majesty sends her congratulations on the completion of the telegraph line.
How historic!
Less than a month later, the ocean's salt water ate through the cable. The wires stopped working.
Morse and Field tried again and again to lay cables—without success. In 1866, Field's ship laid cable from Ireland to Canada. On July 27, Morse received a message from Field.
THE CABLE IS LAID AND IS IN PERFECT WORKING ORDER.

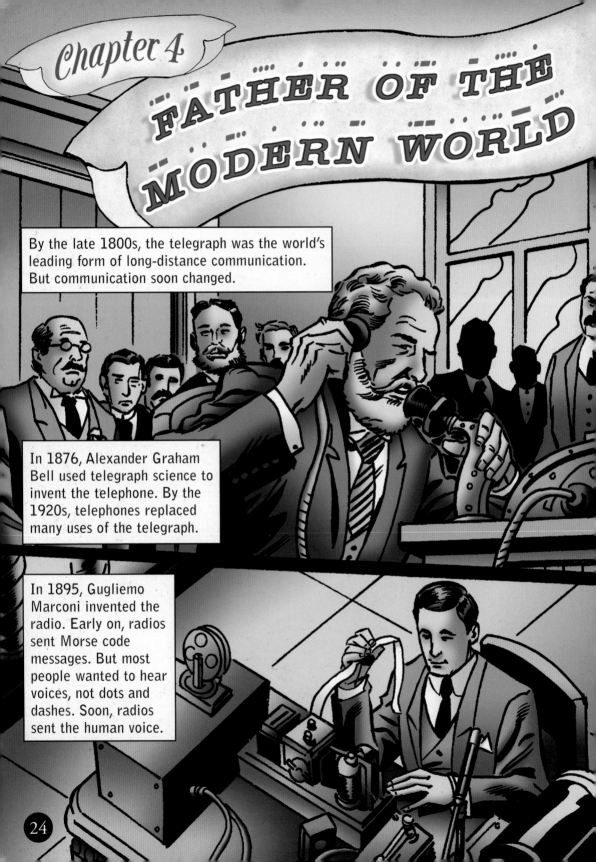

Chapter 4

FATHER OF THE MODERN WORLD

By the late 1800s, the telegraph was the world's leading form of long-distance communication. But communication soon changed.

In 1876, Alexander Graham Bell used telegraph science to invent the telephone. By the 1920s, telephones replaced many uses of the telegraph.

In 1895, Gugliemo Marconi invented the radio. Early on, radios sent Morse code messages. But most people wanted to hear voices, not dots and dashes. Soon, radios sent the human voice.

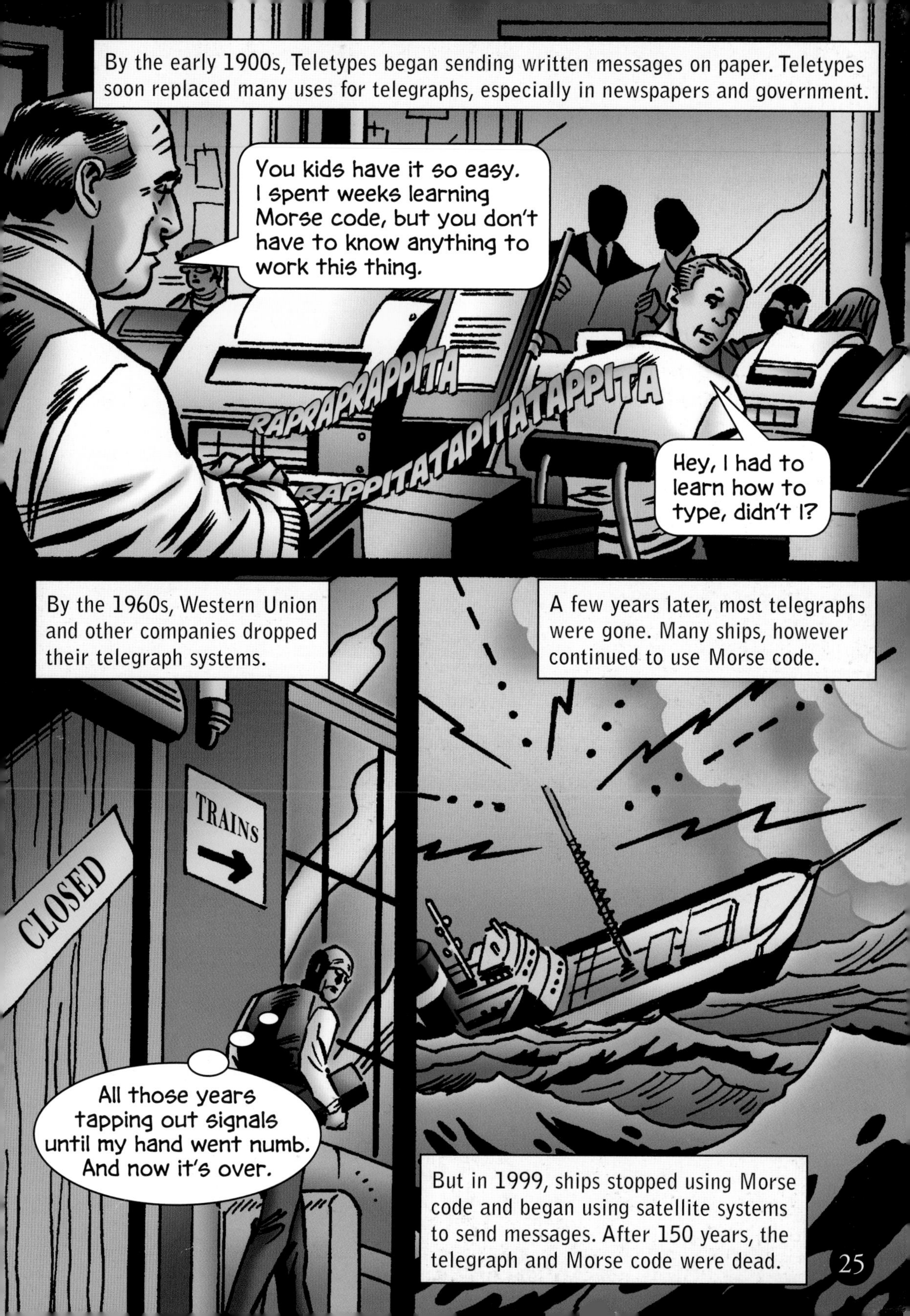
By the early 1900s, Teletypes began sending written messages on paper. Teletypes soon replaced many uses for telegraphs, especially in newspapers and government.
You kids have it so easy. I spent weeks learning Morse code, but you don't have to know anything to work this thing.
RAPRAPRAPPITA
RAPPITATATAPITATAPPITA
Hey, I had to learn how to type, didn't I?
By the 1960s, Western Union and other companies dropped their telegraph systems.
CLOSED
TRAINS
All those years tapping out signals until my hand went numb. And now it's over.
A few years later, most telegraphs were gone. Many ships, however continued to use Morse code.
But in 1999, ships stopped using Morse code and began using satellite systems to send messages. After 150 years, the telegraph and Morse code were dead.

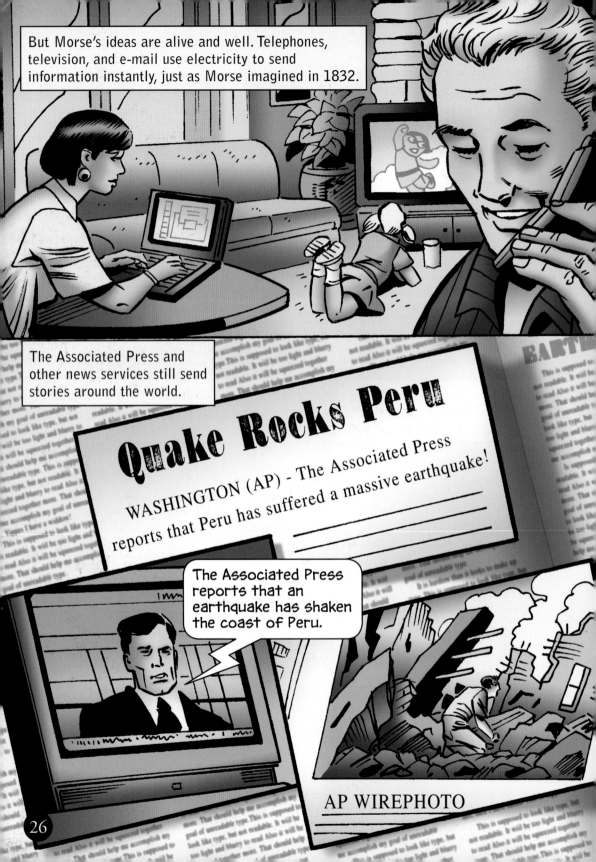

But Morse's ideas are alive and well. Telephones, television, and e-mail use electricity to send information instantly, just as Morse imagined in 1832.

The Associated Press and other news services still send stories around the world.

Quake Rocks Peru

WASHINGTON (AP) - The Associated Press reports that Peru has suffered a massive earthquake!

The Associated Press reports that an earthquake has shaken the coast of Peru.

AP WIREPHOTO

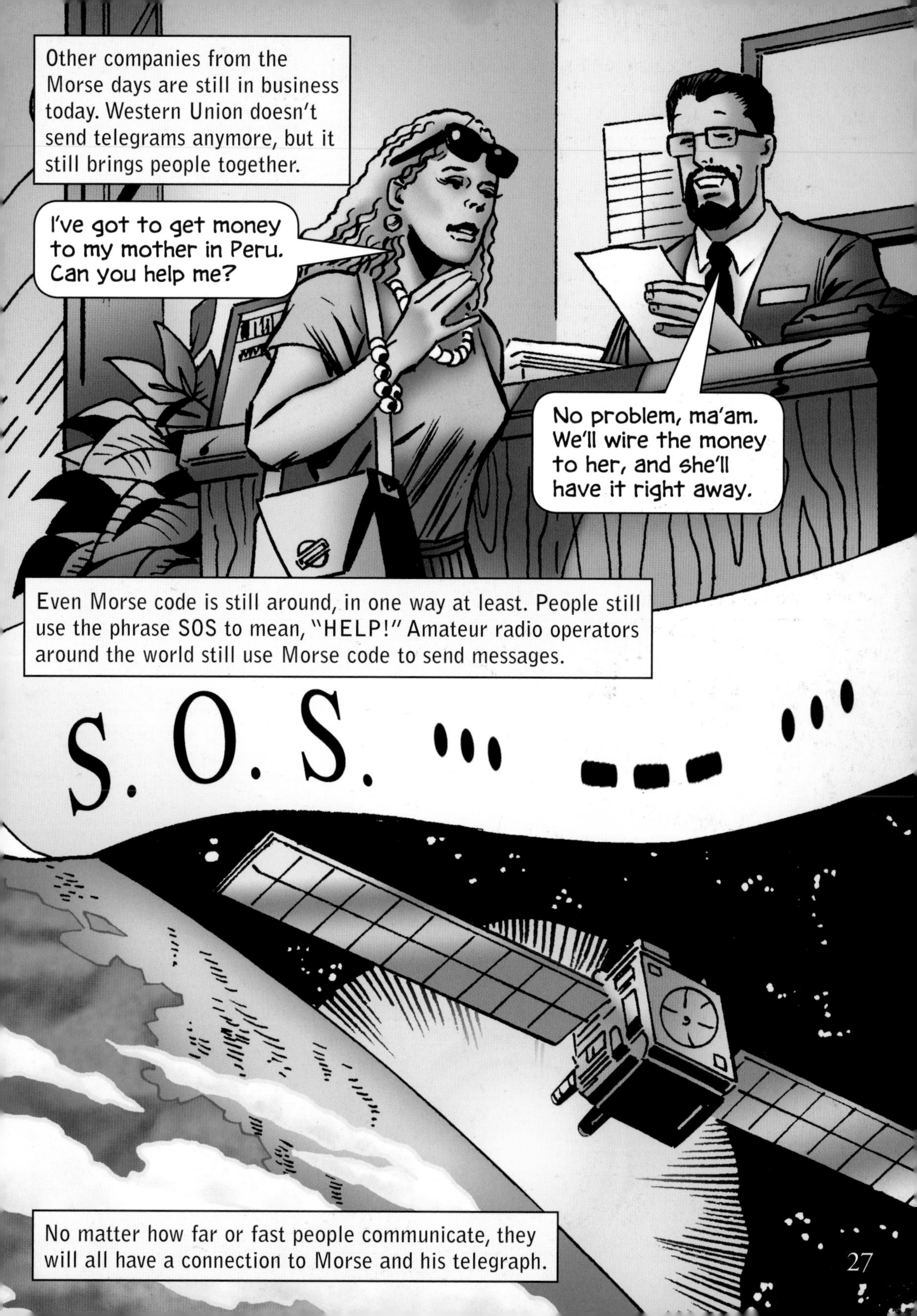

Other companies from the Morse days are still in business today. Western Union doesn't send telegrams anymore, but it still brings people together.
I've got to get money to my mother in Peru. Can you help me?
No problem, ma'am. We'll wire the money to her, and she'll have it right away.
Even Morse code is still around, in one way at least. People still use the phrase SOS to mean, "HELP!" Amateur radio operators around the world still use Morse code to send messages.
S.O.S.
No matter how far or fast people communicate, they will all have a connection to Morse and his telegraph.

More about Morse and the TELEGRAPH

- Samuel Morse was born April 27, 1791, in Charlestown, Massachusetts. He died April 2, 1872, in New York City, at age 80.

- As an artist, Morse was hired to paint portraits of many world leaders, including President James Monroe and Marquis de Lafayette of France.

- Morse was one of the first photographers in the United States. He learned about photography from its inventor, Frenchman Louis Daguerre, on a trip to Europe in the late 1830s.

- The first American telegraph didn't come from Morse. In the late 1820s, inventor Harrison Gray Dyar built a telegraph on Long Island, New York. The telegraph didn't work well, and Dyar gave up on the machine. In 1831, Princeton University science professor Joseph Henry built his own telegraph, but he didn't try to make it link cities as Morse did.

- In the late-1800s, thousands of women worked as telegraph operators. A telegraph operator was one of the few acceptable jobs available to women at that time.

- During the U.S. Civil War (1861–1865), armies for the North and South used telegraphs to relay information. For the first time, commanders received information about the war directly from the battlefields.

- On October 24, 1861, a telegraph line from the east met one from the west in Salt Lake City, Utah. America's east and west coasts were connected for the first time.

- In the 1800s, no one agreed on the correct time. A clock in one city might not show the same time as a clock in another city. In 1865, the United States Naval Observatory started sending the exact time by telegraph. The new system put the entire nation on the same schedule.

- Thomas Edison, one of America's greatest inventors, started out as a telegraph operator. Some of his earliest inventions were improvements on the telegraph.

GLOSSARY

circuit (SUR-kit)—the complete path of an electrical current

current (KUR-uhnt)—the movement of electricity through a wire or other conductor

electromagnet (e-lek-troh-MAG-nit)—a temporary magnet formed when electricity flows through a coil of wire

invest (in-VEST)—to give or lend money to a company

Morse code (MORSS KODE)—a system of dots and dashes used by the telegraph

relay (REE-lay)—an electromagnetic device in which the opening or closing of one circuit operates another device

rival (RYE-vuhl)—someone whom a person competes against

semaphore (SEM-uh-for)—a system of sending messages using flags

INTERNET SITES

FactHound offers a safe, fun way to find Internet sites related to this book. All of the sites on FactHound have been researched by our staff.

Here's how:
1. Visit *www.facthound.com*
2. Choose your grade level.
3. Type in this book ID **0736868461** for age-appropriate sites. You may also browse subjects by clicking on letters, or by clicking on pictures and words.
4. Click on the **Fetch It** button.

FactHound will fetch the best sites for you!

READ MORE

Alter, Judy. *Samuel F. B. Morse: Inventor and Code Creator.* Our People. Chanhassen, Minn: Child's World, 2003.

Hall, M. C. *Samuel Morse.* Lives and Times. Chicago: Heinemann, 2004.

McCormick, Anita Louise. *The Invention of the Telegraph and Telephone in American History.* In American History. Berkeley Heights, N.J.: Enslow, 2004.

Zannos, Susan. *Samuel Morse, and the Story of the Telegraph.* Uncharted, Unexplored, and Unexplained. Hockessin, Del.: Mitchell Lane, 2005.

BIBLIOGRAPHY

Mabee, Carlton. *The American Leonardo: A Life of Samuel F. B. Morse.* New York: A. A. Knopf, 1943.

Morse, Edward Lind, editor. *Samuel F. B. Morse: His Letters and Journals.* Boston: Houghton Mifflin, 1914.

Samuel F. B. Morse Papers at the Library of Congress (http://memory.loc.gov/ammem/sfbmhtml/sfbmhome.html).

Silverman, Kenneth. *Lightning Man: The Accursed Life of Samuel F. B. Morse.* New York: Alfred A. Knopf, 2003.

Telegraph History (http://www.telegraph-history.org).

INDEX

Associated Press, 20, 26

Bell, Alexander Graham, 24
Buchanan, James, 23

communication, 4–5, 6, 8,
    26–27

Dana, James, 7
Day, Jeremiah, 6

electromagnet, 7, 9, 10
Ellsworth, Annie, 15, 16
Ellsworth, Henry, 15

Field, Cyrus, 23
Frederick, King of Denmark,
    22

Gale, Leonard, 13

Henry, Joseph, 10, 19, 28

International Morse code, 22

Jackson, Charles, 9, 10–11,
    19

Madison, James, 5
Marconi, Gugliemo, 24
Minot, Charles, 21

Morse, Lucretia, 7, 8
Morse, Samuel
    as artist, 6–7, 8, 28
    birth of, 28
    death of, 28
    invents telegraph, 10–17
    sends first message, 17
Morse code, 11, 12, 14, 17,
    19, 22, 24, 25, 27

radios, 24, 27
railroads, 21
relay, 13

semaphore, 9, 15

telegraph
    end of, 24–25
    popularity of, 18, 19
    uses of, 18, 20, 21, 29
telephones, 24, 26
Teletype, 25
transatlantic cable, 22–23

Vail, Albert, 13, 14, 16, 17,
    18, 19
Victoria, Queen of England,
    23

Western Union, 20, 25, 27

[redacted] Burgan, Michael.

Goldberg

[redacted]

DATE DUE	BORROWER'S NAME	ROOM NUMBER

[redacted]

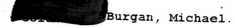

Burgan, Michael.

Goldberg

[redacted]

PTS: 0.5

Quiz: 51160

Lexile:

[redacted]